SCHOLASTIC

Solve-the-Problem Mini-Books

ADDITION & SUBTRACTION

12 Math Stories for Real-World Problem Solving

by Nancy Belkov

Editor: Lynne M. Wilson
Cover design: Mina Chen
Interior design: Grafica Inc.
Illustrations: Steliyana Doneva

ISBN: 978-1-338-80456-0
Scholastic Inc., 557 Broadway, New York, NY 10012
Copyright © 2023 by Nancy Belkov
Published by Scholastic Inc. All rights reserved.
Printed in the U.S.A.
First printing, January 2023.

1 2 3 4 5 6 7 8 9 10   40   32 31 30 29 28 27 26 25 24 23

Table of Contents

Introduction **4**

Math Story Mini-Books

Classroom Visitors *(adding to find the result)* **7**

Too Many Stuffies *(subtracting to find the result)* **13**

Hatching Butterflies *(finding the missing addend)* **19**

The Class Fundraiser
(adding to find the starting number) **25**

The Tree Display *(finding the difference)* **31**

Canned Food Drive *(comparing to find the difference)* **37**

Running Altogether *(finding the smaller unknown)* **43**

Pocket Money *(finding two addends)* **49**

Planning a Trip *(finding the total)* **55**

Science and Fiction *(finding the larger unknown)* **61**

The Notebooks *(finding the missing subtrahend)* **67**

Daily Challenge *(finding the starting number)* **73**

Answer Key **79**

Introduction:
Why Use Stories at Math Time?

Stories invite readers to make connections and try out new ways of thinking. The stories in *Solve-the-Problem Mini-Books* give students opportunities to observe characters who are like them solve real-world math problems together. The characters model asking questions, trying out ideas, taking risks, identifying mistakes, and justifying their thinking. Their example will help students discover new thought processes that will help them make sense of math concepts and solve problems thoughtfully.

Making sense of problems and persevering in solving them is vital to students' success. This key math standard is the backbone of this book. Research shows the effectiveness of teaching math concepts through problem solving.[1] To employ this approach, challenge students with unfamiliar problems that are within their grasp without telling them how to find an answer. Instead of mandating use of a specific operation or strategy, encourage students to try a variety of approaches and strategies independently. Guide them to apply prior knowledge to find solution paths. As students work together to share ideas and strategies, provide them with prompts, questions, ideas, and materials to support their learning. This approach helps students develop confidence and make connections among math concepts.

Learning problem-solving skills takes time. Just as reading regularly helps students become better readers, seeing and doing math regularly helps them understand and become more confident with math. Embed problem solving in relatable contextual situations to help students see math around them and apply new skills in daily life. Use the stories in this book to help make the connection between problem solving and concept learning more symbiotic and to help students develop as problem solvers.

What's in This Book?

In this book you'll find 12 mini-books and companion practice pages that focus primarily on addition and subtraction concepts and skills. These give students a problem-solving model and opportunities to apply the representations and strategies demonstrated by the characters.

Each mini-book presents a contextual problem, focusing on one of the different types of problems identified by Carpenter, Fennema, Franke, Levi, and Empson.[2] These include finding an unknown result, an unknown change, and an unknown starting number through adding, subtracting, and comparing. Many students struggle to understand these kinds of problems, so exposure to all problem types is important.

---

[1] National Council of Teachers of Mathematics (NCTM). (2010, April 8). *Why Is Teaching With Problem Solving Important to Student Learning?* [Research Brief]

[2] Carpenter, T. P., Fennema, E., Franke, M. L., Levi, L., & Empson, S. B. (2014). *Children's Mathematics: Cognitively Guided Instruction, Second Edition*, Heinemann.

How to Use the Mini-Books

Integrating these materials into your current math curriculum is easy. As you plan lessons, consider whether your students have prior knowledge that will enable them to relate to new strategies and concepts in the stories. If you use a curriculum in which students already engage with the problem structures in this book, you may want to use the materials selectively, revisiting problem-solving situations with which your students struggle. A chart of the problem-solving strategies modeled in each mini-book is included in the answer key at the back of the book.

Each mini-book begins with a situational math problem that the student characters must solve. This is followed by "Think" questions, which are designed to help your students learn to read a problem many times (three times is often optimal) to make sense of three essentials:

1) the situation of the problem
2) the question the problem is asking
3) the important information needed to answer the question

Taking time to answer these fundamental questions helps students learn processes for making sense of math problems throughout their work as problem solvers and should become an automatic part of their problem solving.

Create the mini-book. Make double-sided copies of the mini-book so that page 2 appears directly behind the title page. Stack the pages in order and staple along the left side.

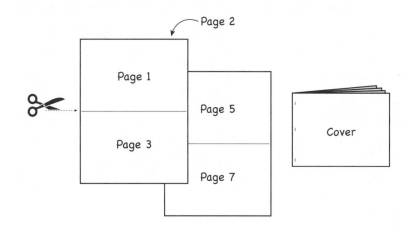

Introduce the mini-book. Students often learn best from other children, so you might introduce a story by saying something like: *Let's see how other students have been solving problems similar to the ones we've been working on.* Project the problem (mini-book page 1) while covering the "Think" questions. Read the problem aloud.

Understand the situation. Uncover the first "Think" question. Successful problem solvers employ a variety of techniques for understanding the problem, including rereading, visualizing, or retelling. Encourage students to try one of the following ways to understand the situation:

• Turn to a partner and describe the situation to each other.
• Draw a picture or diagram to illustrate the situation.
• Act out the situation.

Flexibility with a variety of strategies can help students make sense of problems. Students may use several techniques together or find that one is enough. Facilitate a class share to clarify what is happening in the problem.

Restate the question. Distribute copies of the mini-book. Focusing only on the first page, have students reread the problem and then restate the question in their own words.

Identify the important information. Ask students to identify the information they will need to solve the problem. Discuss why this information is important. Give students the opportunity to think about different ways to use the information, prior knowledge, and modeling tools that might help them solve the problem.

Solve the problem. Students are now ready to think about solution strategies. With some mini-books, you may want students to work in pairs or independently to come up with possible solutions before reading the rest of the story. With others, you may decide to have students move directly to observing how the characters in the story work to solve the problem.

As students read the rest of the story, they will need to process the concepts and strategies the characters use. Whether you use the story as a read-aloud or independent reading, be sure to provide time for discussion and retelling. Encourage students to stop along the way to describe the work the characters do, discuss questions that arise, and try out strategies for themselves. Prompt students to observe how the characters collaborate to solve unfamiliar problems, try out different concepts and strategies, model problems, and reason.

Reflect on the strategies. The last page of each mini-book has "Your Turn" questions to help students analyze the strategies the characters used. These questions provide an opportunity for students to internalize the approaches modeled and clarify underlying math concepts.

Apply the strategies. Finally, use the practice pages to give students the opportunity to try the strategies. These problems encourage students to use at least two problem-solving strategies for each scenario. This promotes self-checking, helps students draw connections, and adds to their tool kits. Have students work independently or in pairs, followed by a class share to address concepts, questions, or struggles.

Classroom Visitors

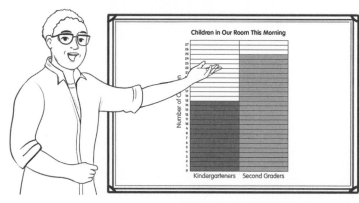

Kindergarten students visited Mr. Smith's second-grade classroom. After they left, Mr. Smith drew a bar graph. He asked his class: *How many students were in our room this morning?*

Think

- What is happening in this story?

- What do the students need to figure out?

- What is the important information?

"Do we count all those boxes to figure out how many students were here?" Tyler asked Kayla.

"No," answered Kayla. "Remember the last time we used a bar graph? Just look at the numbers on the side. 15 is the number at the top of all the darker boxes. That means 15 kindergarteners came."

"I remember now," said Tyler. "The lighter boxes show the 25 second graders. One box for each of us. Then we put 15 and 25 together to find out how many students were in the room."

Mr. Smith's Bar Graph

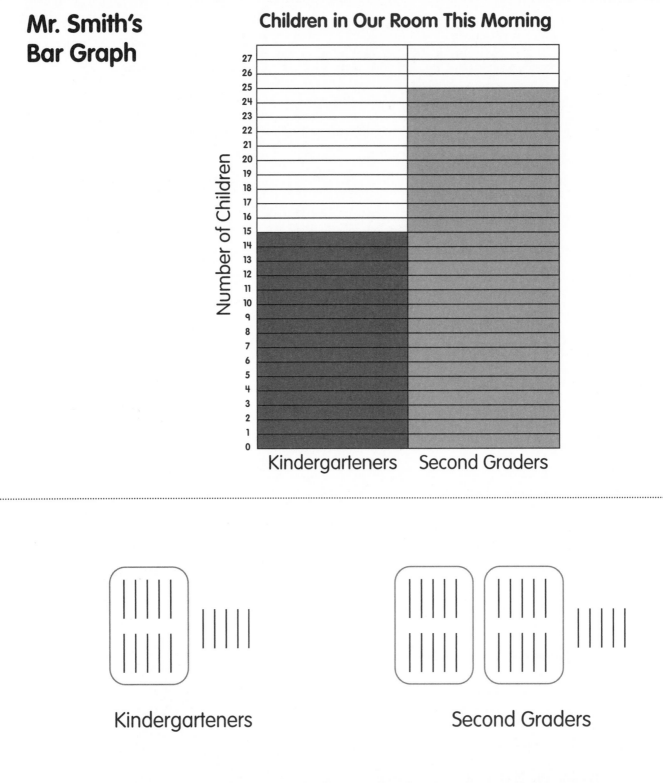

Children in Our Room This Morning

Number of Children

Kindergarteners   Second Graders

Kindergarteners   Second Graders

Tyler drew a bundle of 10 sticks next to 5 separate sticks to show the kindergarteners. Then he drew sticks for the second-grade students. He counted the bundles by tens. Then he counted the ones.

"I think there were 40 students altogether. Do you agree?" asked Tyler.

"I think so," answered Kayla. "Let's put markers in ten frames to check. We can use 10 + 5 markers for the kindergarteners. Then we can use 20 + 5 markers for the second graders."

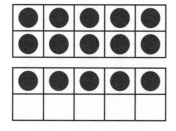

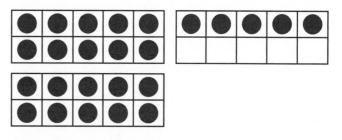

Kindergarteners   Second Graders

"That is like my stick drawings. There are 5 boxes in each of your rows, and I made 5 sticks in each of my rows," said Tyler.

"Yes. Or we can add the tens first, then the ones," said Kayla.

"Great. I can even add 30 + 10 in my head. 3 tens and 1 more ten make 40," said Tyler.

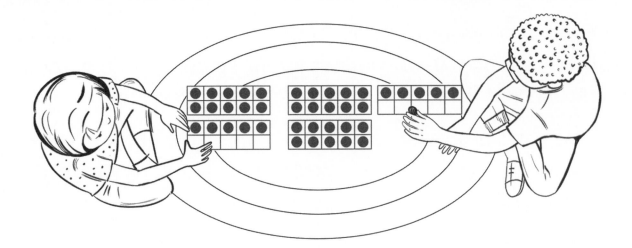

"Yes. A full ten frame has 10 things because 5 + 5 = 10. Let's start with the 25 second graders. Then we'll add on the 15 kindergarteners," said Kayla.

"Okay, 25 plus 5 more is 30. Then add on one more 10. That equals 40. Right?" asked Tyler.

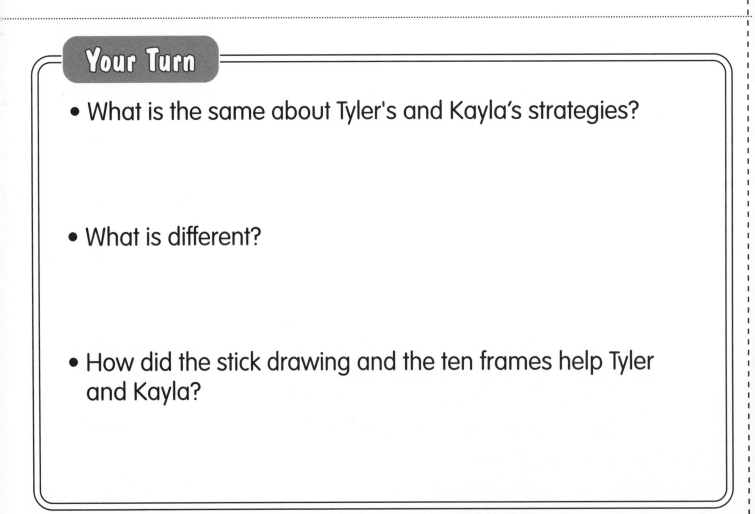

Your Turn

- What is the same about Tyler's and Kayla's strategies?

- What is different?

- How did the stick drawing and the ten frames help Tyler and Kayla?

Name: _____

Adding to Find the Result

Here are more problems. Think about what you know about tens and ones. Try to use the strategies Tyler and Kayla used to solve their problem.

1. Mr. Smith's class made birthday cards to sell at the school fundraiser. They made 24 cards on Monday. On Tuesday they made 32 more cards. How many cards did they have to sell?

2. Luis collects erasers of different sizes and colors. He had 41 erasers in his collection. His cousin gave him 16 new erasers. How many erasers does he have now?

3. Bonnie saves the pictures she paints in a folder. She had 53 pictures in her folder in the morning. She brought 25 new pictures home from school. She put them in her folder. How many pictures are in her folder now?

4. David's class had 62 books in their class library. Then their teacher put 27 new books in the class library. How many books are in their library now?

Extension: Change the numbers in one of the problems above or make your own problem. Solve your problem.

Too Many Stuffies

Mr. Smith's daughter had 62 stuffed animals. She thought she had too many. So she gave 31 of them to her brother. Mr. Smith asked his students: *How many stuffed animals does my daughter have now?*

Think

- What is happening in this story?

- What do the students need to figure out?

- What is the important information?

Ben also made a drawing. He drew all the animals. Then he crossed out 31 of them.

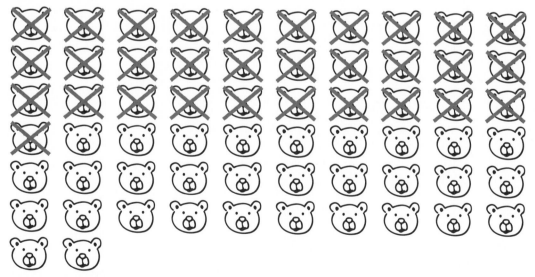

"I see 31 left in both of your drawings," said Amber. "We can use an open number line to check our work."

Tony drew sticks and dots to show the 62 animals. He drew a stick for each group of ten animals. He drew a dot for each one. He drew 6 sticks and 2 dots.

Next, Tony crossed out sticks and dots to show the 31 animals that Mr. Smith's daughter gave away. He crossed out 3 sticks and 1 dot. He shared his diagram with his partners, Amber and Ben.

Stuffed Animals

||||| • •
|

XXX|| ✗ •
|

"Let's take away 31 on the number line. We should get 31 again," Amber said. "We can start by jumping back 30 from 62."

"How can we take away a big number like 30 all at once?" asked Ben.

"It's just like my sticks," answered Tony. "We take tens from tens. We start at 62. When we take away 3 tens, we have 3 tens and 2 ones left."

"I get it," said Ben. "Then we just have to take away the 1."

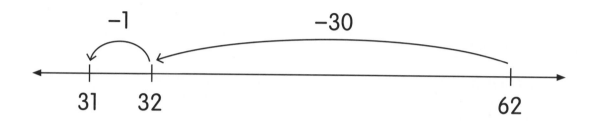

"It helps me too," said Ben. "If you add two numbers together, you get the total. When you take one of the numbers away from that total, you get the other number. Since I remember more addition facts, I use them to help me subtract."

"Oh! So, to figure out 62 − 31, I think about how much to add to 31 to get 62," Tony said. "31 + __ = 62. Thanks for the tip. That makes subtraction easier."

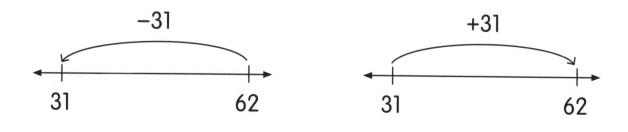

"That number line reminds me of a double we can use to get the same answer," Amber said. "I know that 30 + 30 = 60, so 31 + 31 = 62."

"Wait, why did you use addition?" asked Tony, confused. "We need to take some away."

"Yes, but addition helps me with subtraction," said Amber.

Your Turn

- How did Tony, Ben, and Amber use tens and ones to solve their problem?

- How did they use an addition problem to help them solve their problem?

Name: _____

Subtracting to Find the Result

Here are some problems to solve. Try to use the strategies Tony, Amber, and Ben used to solve their problem. Solve each problem in at least two different ways.

1. The second-grade class had 28 tulip bulbs to plant. They planted 14 tulip bulbs in the front of the school. How many tulip bulbs did they have left to plant in the back of the school?

2. Sam found 25 nickels on the ground. He put 12 of those nickels in his piggy bank. He put the rest of the nickels in his pocket to take to the store. How many nickels did he take to the store?

3. Tiana's mother bought 52 boxes of juice. She put 26 of them on the table for a party. She put the rest of the boxes in the cabinet. How many boxes of juice did she put in the cabinet?

4. Ms. Jones took 43 pictures out of a box. She hung them on the wall. Before she started, the box had 84 pictures in it. How many pictures were in the box after she hung up pictures?

Extension: Change the numbers in one of the problems above or make your own problem. Solve your problem.

Hatching Butterflies

Solve-the-Problem Mini-Books: Addition & Subtraction © Nancy Belkov, Scholastic Inc.

Mr. Smith's class is studying butterflies. Last year's class hatched a record 30 butterflies from caterpillars. This year's class has hatched 17 so far. The students asked: *To match the record, how many more butterflies do we need to hatch?*

Think

- What is happening in this story?

- What do the students need to figure out?

- What is the important information?

"Does this diagram help?" asked Elijah. "It shows last year's butterflies. Then it shows the ones we have so far. And there's space to show that we don't know how many more we need."

Elijah's Diagram

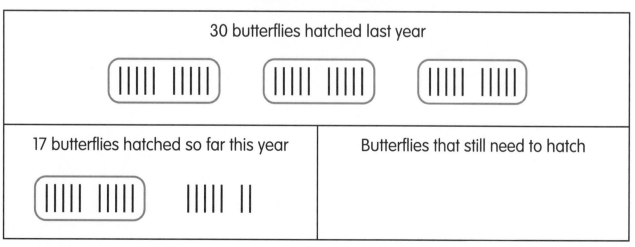

"How many more butterflies need to hatch?" Sarah asked Elijah. "I don't know how to figure that out."

"That helps," Sarah said. "We can start with the number they hatched last year. Then take away the butterflies we've hatched so far this year." She started writing.

30 - 17 = ?
30 - 10 = 20
20 - 7 = 13

"Why did you subtract? Don't take any beautiful butterflies away!" said Elijah. "We need to add butterflies. We already have 17. I'll use lighter color sticks to see how many more we'll need to get to 30 butterflies."

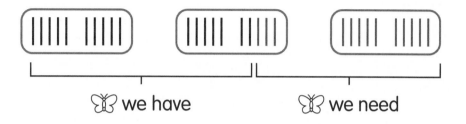

🦋 we have   🦋 we need

"I like how you used a different color," said Sarah. "I can easily see that you drew 13 more. That's what I got when I subtracted!"

"Your number line shows we need 13 more caterpillars to hatch," said Sarah. "So does my number line when I jump back 17."

Sarah's Number Line

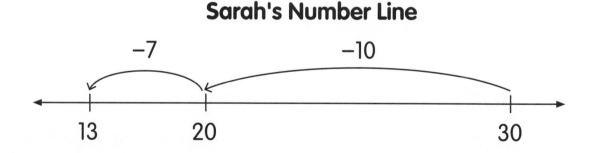

"We get the same answer! That's because there are two parts to the total number of butterflies we want to have," said Elijah. "There are the ones we've hatched. And there are the ones we still need. So, if we remove either one of the parts, the other part is left."

"Why did we get the same answer adding or subtracting?" Elijah asked. "I'll try an open number line. Let's see if I get 13 when I add. Because 17 butterflies have already hatched, I start at 17. Next, I jump 3 to get to 20. Finally, I jump 10 to get to 30."

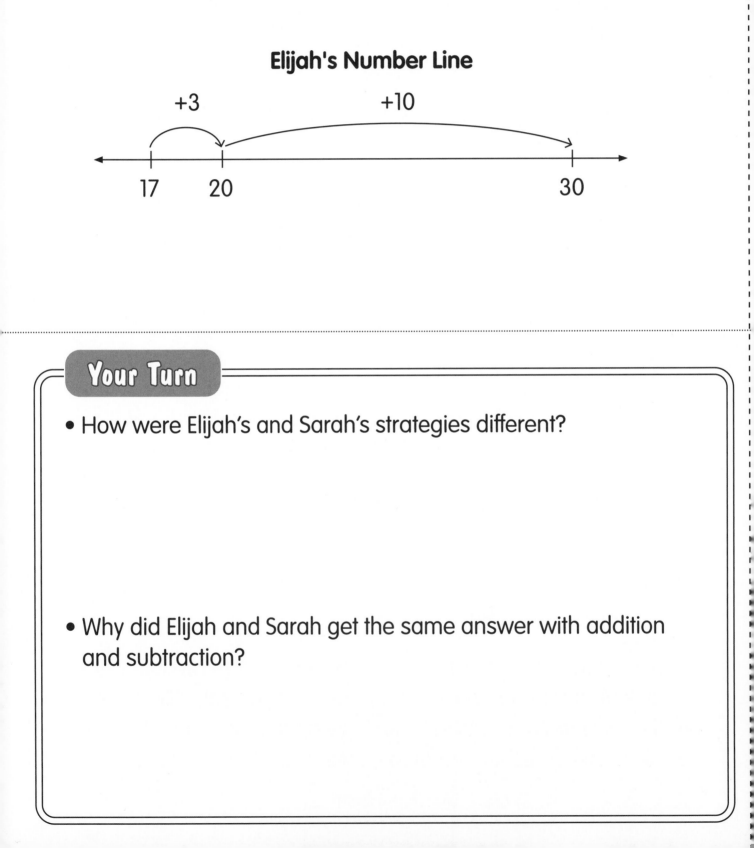

Elijah's Number Line

+3   +10

17   20   30

Your Turn

- How were Elijah's and Sarah's strategies different?

- Why did Elijah and Sarah get the same answer with addition and subtraction?

Name: _____

Finding the Missing Addend

Here are some problems to solve. Try to use the strategies Elijah and Sarah used to solve their problem. Solve each problem in at least two different ways.

1. Sam's brother has 14 puppets. Sam only has 8 puppets. How many more puppets would Sam need to have as many puppets as his brother has?

2. Jasmine can fit 34 beads on a bracelet. She is making a bracelet for her grandma. She has put 18 beads on the bracelet. How many more beads can she put on her grandma's bracelet?

3. Carmen wants to jump rope for 60 seconds without stopping. Her record for jumping rope is 45 seconds. How many more seconds would she have needed to jump to reach her goal?

4. David has read 52 books so far this year. He wants to read 70 books by the end of the year. How many more books does he need to read?

Extension: Change the numbers in one of the problems above or make your own problem. Solve your problem.

The Class Fundraiser

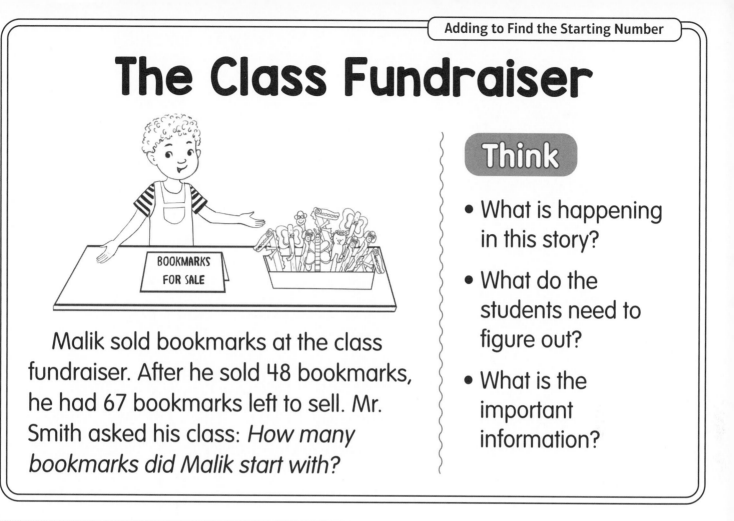

Malik sold bookmarks at the class fundraiser. After he sold 48 bookmarks, he had 67 bookmarks left to sell. Mr. Smith asked his class: *How many bookmarks did Malik start with?*

Think

- What is happening in this story?

- What do the students need to figure out?

- What is the important information?

"Malik must have started with some bookmarks," said Kayla. "After he sold 48 of them, he had 67 left. We have to figure out how many he had when he started. I mean, before he sold 48 bookmarks." She showed Trevor this picture:

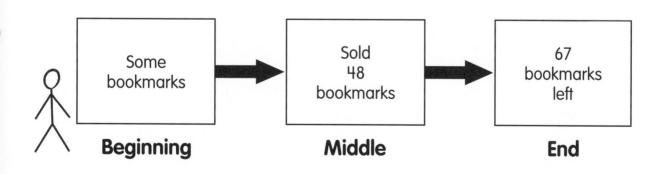

Some bookmarks	Sold 48 bookmarks	67 bookmarks left
Beginning	**Middle**	**End**

"I am trying to picture this story in my head. I know it's about selling bookmarks. But I can't imagine how it starts. I know Malik sold 48 of them. But what happened first?" Trevor asked Kayla.

"Yes, Malik had more in the beginning," said Trevor. "He had the 48 he sold, and he had the 67 that were left. Let's use pictures to add. I'll draw sticks for tens and dots for ones."

"That shows why we add 48 and 67," said Kayla. "Let's add the tens then the ones."

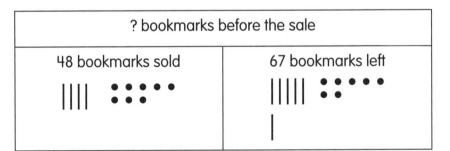

$$48 + 67 = ?$$

$$40 + 60 = 100$$

$$8 + 7 = 15$$

$$100 + 15 = 115$$

"Let's try an open number line," said Trevor. "We should get 115 bookmarks if we start with 67 and add on 48. Let's add in chunks. First, I'll add 3 and get to 70. Then add 30 to get to 100. And finally, add the other ten and the ones."

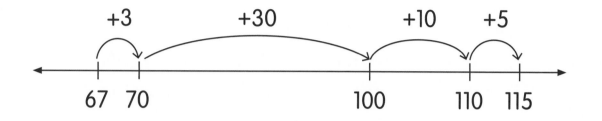

"I'm glad you remembered to add the rest of the ones at the end," Kayla said. "And we did get 115 that way too!"

"Okay," said Kayla. "So, we break 65 into 50 + 15. Then we add the parts." She wrote:

$$50 + 65 = ?$$
$$50 + (50 + 15) = ?$$
$$50 + 50 = 100$$
$$100 + 15 = 115$$

"We got the same answer 3 different ways!" said Trevor.

bookmarks sold

bookmarks left

Trevor said, "I thought of another strategy. Pretend Malik sold 50 instead of 48. And pretend that he had 65 left instead of 67."

"Why would you change the numbers?" asked Kayla.

"It is easier to add 50 and 65. We know that 50 + 50 = 100," answered Trevor. "So, I just moved 2 of the ones he sold to the ones he had left. The total number of bookmarks is still the same."

Your Turn

- How did Kayla's diagram help Trevor and Kayla?

- How are the students' three strategies the same? How are they different?

Name: _____

Adding to Find the Starting Number

Here are some problems to solve. Try to use the strategies Trevor and Kayla used to solve their problem. Solve each problem in at least two different ways.

1. A school bus driver drove children to school. After 26 children got off the bus, there were still 38 children on the bus. How many children were on the bus before any got off it?

2. Tasha sold homemade bracelets at the fundraiser. She sold 89 bracelets. She had 24 bracelets left at the end of the sale. How many bracelets did she have before the sale?

3. A librarian had some books on his cart. He took 79 books from his cart. He put those books on the shelves. Then he had 64 books left on the cart. How many books were on his cart before he put the books on shelves?

4. A farmer was selling boxes of eggs from her truck. After she sold 58 boxes of eggs, she had 97 boxes left in her truck. How many boxes of eggs did she have before she sold the 58 boxes?

Extension: Change the numbers in one of the problems above or make your own problem. Solve your problem.

The Tree Display

Zoe and Adam made a model oak tree. It measured 74 inches tall. The trunk of the tree was 28 inches tall. Mr. Smith asked: *How tall the is the crown of the tree?*

Think

- What is happening in this story?

- What do the students need to figure out?

- What is the important information?

"I like your picture. It helps me think about the height of the crown," said Ben.

"What if we take the height of the trunk away from the whole tree? So we take 28 away from 74," said Mia. "I think the rest of the inches would be the height of the crown."

"Do you think the crown measures 74 inches plus 28 inches?" Ben asked Mia.

"No, the trunk is part of the whole tree. So 28 inches is part of the height," answered Mia. "Let's draw it. We can show the height of the tree is 74 inches. And we can show the trunk is 28 inches."

Mia's drawing

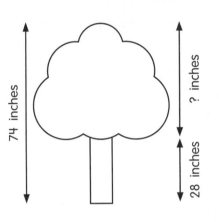

"Yes," said Ben. "Let's use tens frames. Here are 74 dots on tens frames to show the 74 inches. I crossed out 28 dots for the trunk of the tree."

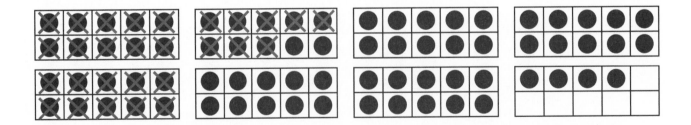

"I also wrote equations to show how I took away the 28," said Ben. "I took it away in chunks."

"Great! Then we add all the jumps. We get 46 this way too. 2 + 40 + 4 = 46," said Ben.

"It's neat that we used both addition and subtraction to solve the problem," said Mia.

"I think that works," Mia said. "Addition should work too. We start with 28 inches for the trunk. Then we find how many inches we need to add to get the total height of 74."

Mia drew an open number line. "Adding on a number line even feels like measuring. It's like a tree lying down," she said.

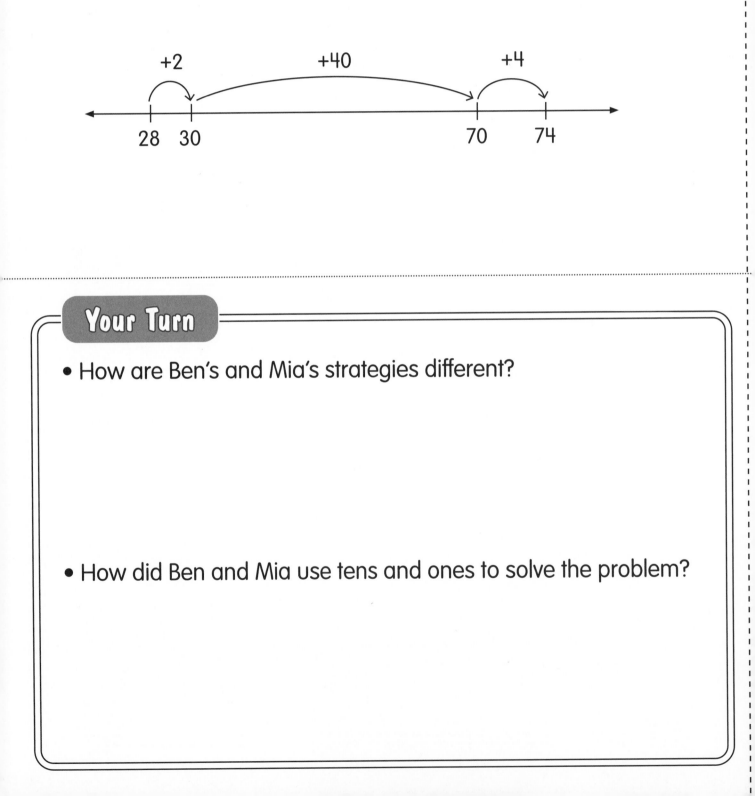

Your Turn

- How are Ben's and Mia's strategies different?

- How did Ben and Mia use tens and ones to solve the problem?

Name: _____

Finding the Difference

Here are some problems to solve. Try to use the strategies Ben and Mia used to solve their problem. Solve each problem in at least two different ways.

1. A pet store put 23 animal photos in their display window. There were 7 pictures of fish. The rest were pictures of dogs. How many pictures of dogs were in the display window?

2. There were 34 floats in the holiday parade. Before the band, there were 19 floats. The rest of the floats came after the band. How many floats came after the band?

3. There were 62 students in the student chorus. Only 28 of the students were in 4th grade. The rest were in 5th grade. How many 5th graders were in the chorus?

4. The school library had 81 chairs. Most of the chairs were made of wood, but 26 of the chairs were plastic. How many of the chairs were made of wood?

Extension: Change the numbers in one of the problems above or make your own problem. Solve your problem.

Canned Food Drive

Mr. Smith's students collected 110 cans of food for the school food drive. Ms. Green's class collected 85 cans. Mr. Smith asked his students: *How many more cans than Ms. Green's class did our class collect?*

Think

- What is happening in this story?

- What do the students need to figure out?

- What is the important information?

"Thanks, Mia," said Elijah. "That makes it easier to see. We collected 85 cans plus some extras. I'll draw a line in the box to show the extras."

Elijah's Diagram

extra cans	
85 cans Mr. Smith's Class	85 cans Ms. Green's class

"You can see in my diagram that our class collected more canned food than Ms. Green's class," Mia said to Elijah.

Mia's Diagram

110 cans
Mr. Smith's
Class

85 cans
Ms. Green's
class

"I think we need to figure out how many more cans we collected after we had 85 cans," said Mia. "Those are our extras."

"I agree. So, first we collected 85 cans," said Elijah. "When we got 5 more cans, we had 90. Then people gave us 10 more. That got us to 100."

$$85 + 5 = 90$$
$$90 + 10 = 100$$
1

"Yes," Mia agreed. "And then we collected 10 more to get to 110. Just like on my number line!"

Mia's Number Line

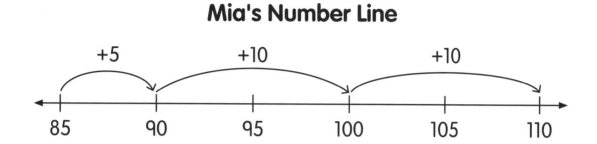

"But we didn't answer the question. Do you think we collected 25 more cans than Ms. Green's class?" asked Mia.

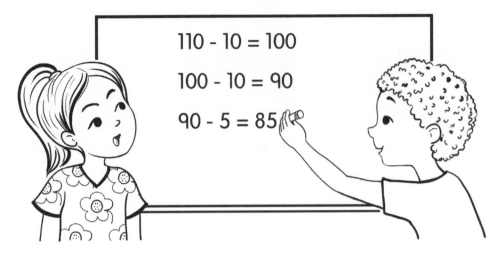

110 - 10 = 100

100 - 10 = 90

90 - 5 = 85

"We could also see how many cans we need to take away from our donations to have the same number as Ms. Green's class," suggested Elijah. "I know 110 – 10 = 100. So first, I'll take away 10. Next, I'll take away 10 more to get to 90. And then just take away 5 more to get to 85."

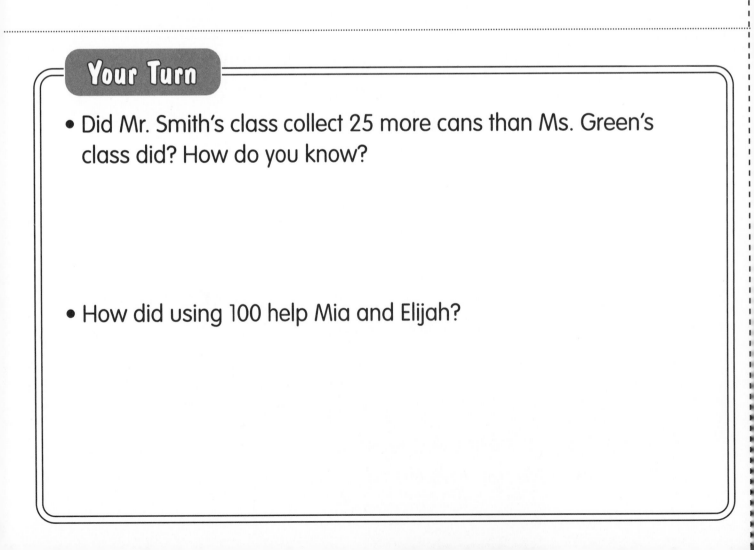

Your Turn

- Did Mr. Smith's class collect 25 more cans than Ms. Green's class did? How do you know?

- How did using 100 help Mia and Elijah?

Name: _____

Comparing to Find the Difference

Here are some problems to solve. Try to use the strategies Mia and Elijah used to solve their problem. Solve each problem in at least two different ways.

1. Brett and Steven collect marbles. Brett has 48 marbles in her collection. Steven has 62 marbles. How many more marbles does Steven have?

2. Min and Jordan live in different states. One year they compared how many days of rain they each got. Min said it rained on 35 days in her town. In Jordan's city, it rained on 72 days. How many fewer rainy days did Min's town have?

3. The second-grade teachers ordered 75 folders for their students. The third-grade teachers ordered 120 folders. How many more folders did the third-grade teachers order?

4. James lives 47 kilometers away from his grandparents. Roberto lives 136 kilometers from his grandparents. How much closer is James to his grandparents?

Extension: Change the numbers in one of the problems above or make your own problem. Solve your problem.

Running Altogether

Solve-the-Problem Mini-Books: Addition & Subtraction © Nancy Belkov, Scholastic Inc.

Mr. Smith's students ran a total of 124 kilometers in October. They ran 12 more kilometers in October than they ran in September. Mr. Smith asked them: *How many kilometers did you run altogether in September?*

Think

- What is happening in this story?

- What do the students need to figure out?

- What is the important information?

"I get it," said Brian. He drew two open number lines. "When we added the kilometers all of us ran for October, it was 124 kilometers altogether. That was more than we ran in September. These number lines show that our total distance in October was more than our total distance in September."

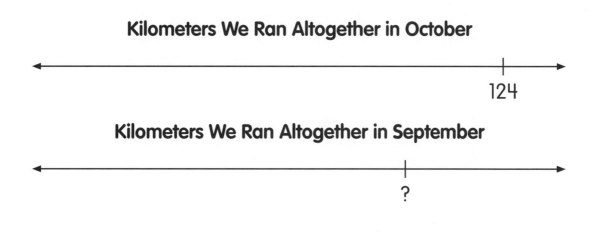

Kilometers We Ran Altogether in October

124

Kilometers We Ran Altogether in September

?

"I'm confused. Mr. Smith said 'altogether,' so do we add?" Brian asked Amber. "If we add 124 + 12 that will be more than we ran in October."

"No," answered Amber. "I think he said 'altogether' because we all put our kilometers together to get the total. Pretend there were just three of us. Say I ran 4 kilometers. You ran 3. And Carlos ran 2. 4 + 3 + 2 = 9. So, that would be 9 kilometers altogether."

"Yes. So, if we knew how much we ran in September, we would start there. We would add 12 to that number and get 124," Amber said. "Our kilometers in September + 12 kilometers = 124 kilometers." She drew a new number line.

Amber's Number Line

"That gives me an idea," said Brian. "Since September's total + 12 = 124, that means 12 + September's total = 124 too. We can start at 12 and see how much we need to add to get to 124."

"Great idea," said Amber. "Let's first jump ahead 100. Then we can keep going."

Brian's Number Line

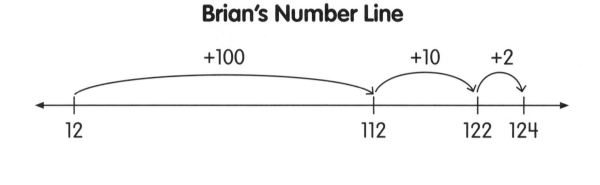

"I can do that subtraction in my head," said Amber. "We don't have any hundreds to take away. 100 − 0 = 100. Then we just take 12 away from 24. So, we ran 112 kilometers in September."

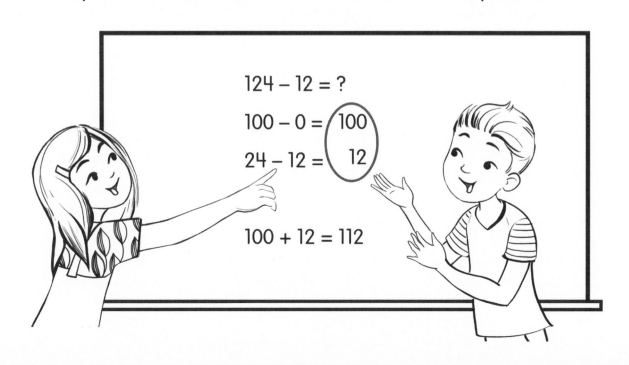

"Or we can take 12 away from 124 with jumps like this," said Brian.

Brian's Subtraction Number Line

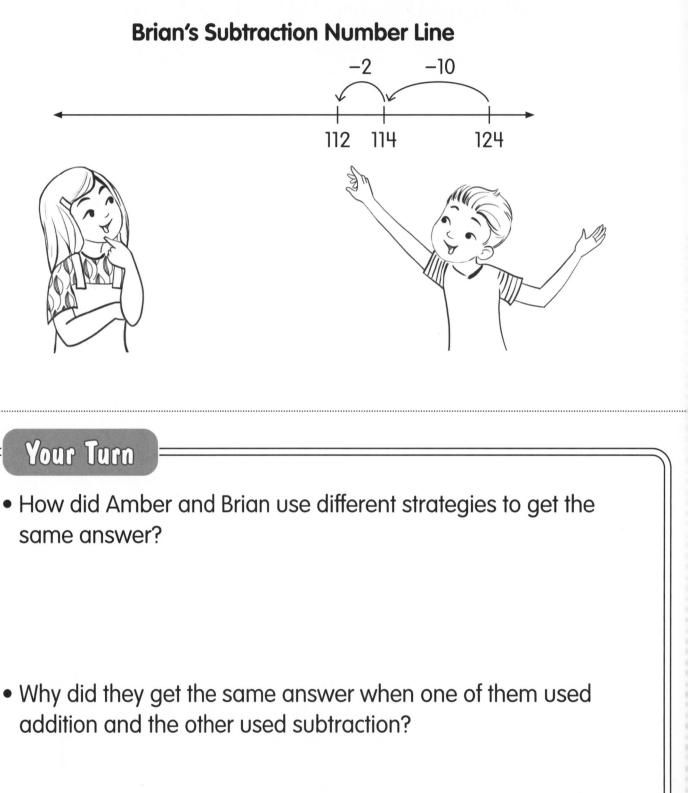

- How did Amber and Brian use different strategies to get the same answer?

- Why did they get the same answer when one of them used addition and the other used subtraction?

Name: _____

Finding the Smaller Unknown

Here are some problems to solve. Try to use the strategies Amber and Brian used to solve their problem. Solve each problem in at least two different ways.

1. Austin and Kai were practicing for a jump-rope contest. Austin jumped 70 seconds. He jumped 25 more seconds than Kai did. How many seconds did Kai jump?

2. Anika and Vincent both counted the houses they walk by on their way to school. Anika walks by 29 more houses than Vincent. She walks by 92 houses. How many houses does Vincent walk by?

3. Gloria read 186 pages of her new chapter book. She read 24 more pages than Mateo. How many pages did Mateo read?

4. Ashley has 18 fewer markers than Jordan has. Jordan has 102 markers. How many markers does Ashley have?

Extension: Change the numbers in one of the problems above or make your own problem. Solve your problem.

Pocket Money

Mr. Smith said that he had at least one nickel and at least one dime in his pocket. He had no other kinds of coins. The coins in his pocket were worth 65 cents. He asked: *What coins might be in my pocket?*

Think

- What is happening in this story?
- What do the students need to figure out?
- What is the important information?

"Do you mean we could try something like 10 dimes to see whether that works?" asked Ben.

"Exactly," Rosa said. "But I think that's too many dimes. Ten dimes is the same as 100 cents, or one dollar. And he said he has at least one nickel. So, why don't we try starting with 1 nickel?"

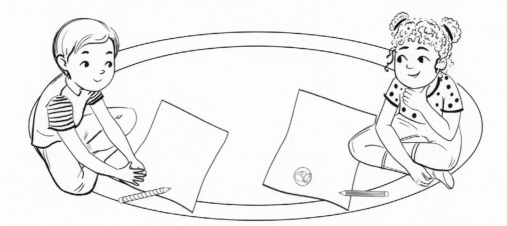

"We don't know how many nickels or how many dimes he has!" Ben said to Rosa. "How can we figure that out?"

"We do know he has 65 cents altogether," Rosa replied. "Let's try some things to see what works."

"Okay," replied Ben. "If he only has one nickel, then the rest of his coins are dimes. Take away the 5 cents: 65 – 5 = 60. So, he has enough dimes to make 60 cents. 6 tens equals 60, so he has 6 dimes."

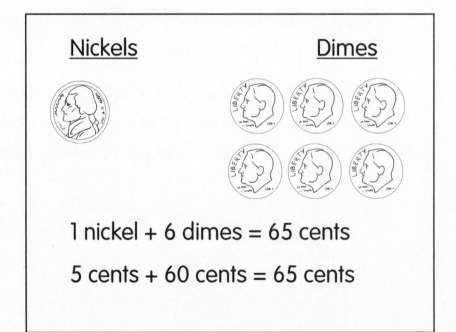

Nickels   Dimes

1 nickel + 6 dimes = 65 cents

5 cents + 60 cents = 65 cents

"I agree. But I also think he could have a different number of dimes and nickels and still have 65 cents," Rosa said. "What if we try 2 nickels instead of 1?"

Ben and Rosa tried to find other ways to make 65 cents.

See if you can find more ways for Mr. Smith to have 65 cents in his pocket. Then read on to see what Ben and Rosa found.

"If he just has to have an odd number of nickels, that means there are even more answers. Let's see how many we can find," said Rosa. She wrote:

Nickels	Dimes	Total
1 for 5 cents	6 for 60 cents	60 + 5 = 65 cents
3 for 15 cents	5 for 50 cents	50 + 15 = 65 cents
5 for 25 cents		

"I guess Mr. Smith couldn't have only 2 nickels with his dimes," said Rosa. "Two nickels is 10 cents. And 65 − 10 = 55. Since dimes are tens, you can't make 55 cents with dimes. But he could have 3 nickels. Look!"

"I agree. He needs to have an odd number of nickels with his dimes to make 65 cents," said Ben.

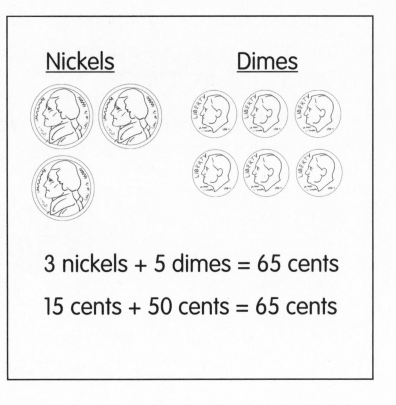

Nickels   Dimes

3 nickels + 5 dimes = 65 cents

15 cents + 50 cents = 65 cents

Your Turn

- Is there another way for Mr. Smith to have 65 cents with at least one dime and at least one nickel? How?

- How does the way that Ben and Rosa organized their work help you find all the possible answers?

Name: _____

Finding Two Addends

Here are some problems to solve. All the problems have more than one right answer. See how many possible answers you can find for each problem.

1. David had 30 cents in his piggy bank. He had some pennies and some nickels. What coins might he have in his piggy bank?

2. The aquarium wants to buy 40 reptiles. They want to buy at least 18 turtles and at least 18 lizards. How many of each can they buy?

3. The school store sells bags of erasers. Each bag has 22 erasers. Each bag has at least 5 strawberry erasers and at least 5 banana erasers. How many of each kind of eraser might be in each bag?

4. Jamie's sister has 80 cents in her pocket. She has some quarters, some nickels, and no other kinds of coins. What coins might she have in her pocket?

Extension: Change the numbers in one of the problems above or make your own problem. Solve your problem.

Planning a Trip

The three second-grade teachers are planning a bus trip. Each bus has 60 passenger seats. Mr. Smith invited 34 people, Ms. Green invited 30 people, and Ms. Felder invited 47 people. Mr. Smith asked his class: *Will everyone fit on 2 buses?*

Think

- What is happening in this story?

- What do the students need to figure out?

- What is the important information?

Bus One

Bus Two

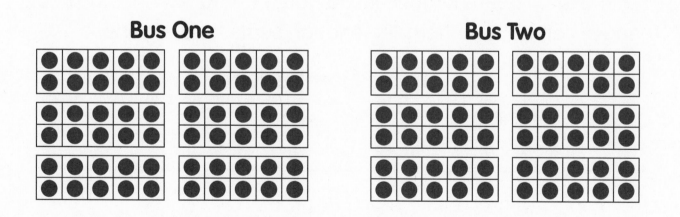

"Each bus has 60 seats. So 2 buses have 120 seats altogether," Andy said. "Think of it as 6 tens plus 6 tens, which makes 12 tens. That's 120."

"Two buses can hold a lot of people. There must be enough room," Theo said to Andy and Olivia.

"I'm not so sure," said Olivia. "Ms. Felder invited 47 people. They will almost fill all the seats in one bus. We need to add 60 plus 60 to see how many seats there will be altogether."

"I'll make an open number line to add 34 + 30 + 47," said Theo. "Then we can be sure there are enough seats for everyone."

Theo's Number Line

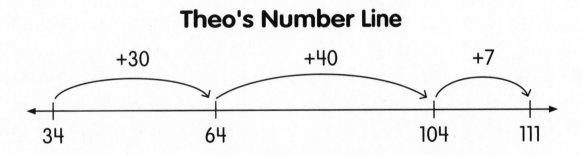

"You jumped by 3 tens, then 4 tens. Why?" asked Olivia.

"It was easier for me to start with Mr. Smith's 34 people and add on Ms. Green's 30 people," answered Theo. "That way, I just had to add 3 tens and 3 tens. The ones stayed the same."

"I can see that you did the same thing when you added 40 onto 64," said Andy. "4 tens plus 6 tens make 10 tens, or 100, and you still had the 4 ones. But where did the 40 come from?"

"I know!" Olivia exclaimed. "Theo broke Ms. Felder's 47 people into 2 chunks. He made one chunk of 40 people and one chunk of 7 people. After he added the 40, he added 7 onto 104. This time both the ones and tens changed since 7 + 4 = 11."

$$47 = 40 + 7$$
$$64 + 40 = 104$$
$$104 + 7 = 111$$

"Great!" said Olivia. "We used two different strategies and still got the same answer. But we forgot to add seats for the teachers!"

"We can use the tens and ones to add another way too," said Andy. "We can break 34 into 30 + 4 and break 47 into 40 + 7. First, we add up the tens, then the ones. Finally, we put together the hundreds, the tens, and the ones."

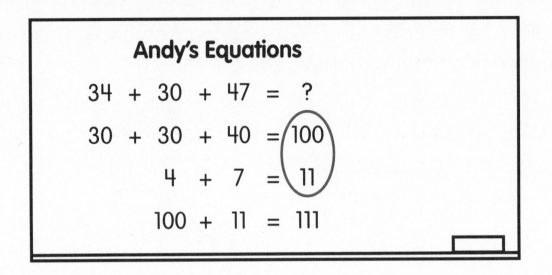

Andy's Equations

$$34 + 30 + 47 = \text{?}$$
$$30 + 30 + 40 = 100$$
$$4 + 7 = 11$$
$$100 + 11 = 111$$

Your Turn

- Will there be enough seats for everyone, including the teachers? How do you know?

- What was different about the two strategies the students used?

Name: _____

Finding the Total

Here are some problems to solve. Each problem has several steps to think about. Try to use the strategies Olivia, Theo, and Andy used to solve their problem. Solve each problem in at least two different ways.

1. Larry is getting ready for his mom's 45th birthday party. He has 17 round balloons and 19 long balloons. Does he have enough balloons to hang 45 balloons?

2. Olivia climbed three sets of stairways on a hike. She counted the steps. The first stairway had 40 steps. The next had 13 steps. Then there was a long stairway with 120 steps. How many steps did she climb altogether?

3. Sam has pens in a jar. They are 4 different colors. Seventeen of the pens are green, 20 are black, 13 are purple, and 30 are blue. How many pens does he have in his jar?

4. Julie is trying to read 100 minutes every week. She read 25 minutes the first day. On the second day she read 32 minutes, and she read 20 minutes on the third day. How many minutes did she read altogether in those three days?

5. Liam collects pennies. He has 149 pennies in a jar. His sister gave him 45 pennies from her piggy bank. Liam wants to exchange his pennies for dollars. He knows 100 pennies make a dollar. Does he have enough pennies to make 2 dollars?

Extension: Change the numbers in one of the problems above or make your own problem. Solve your problem.

Science and Fiction

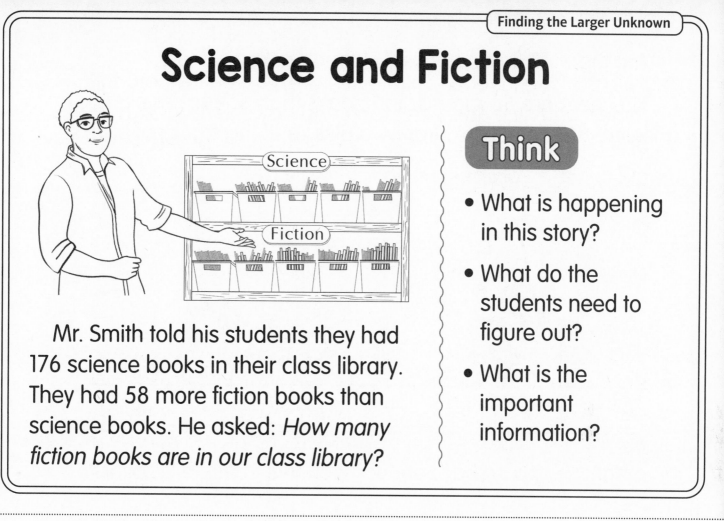

Mr. Smith told his students they had 176 science books in their class library. They had 58 more fiction books than science books. He asked: *How many fiction books are in our class library?*

Think

- What is happening in this story?

- What do the students need to figure out?

- What is the important information?

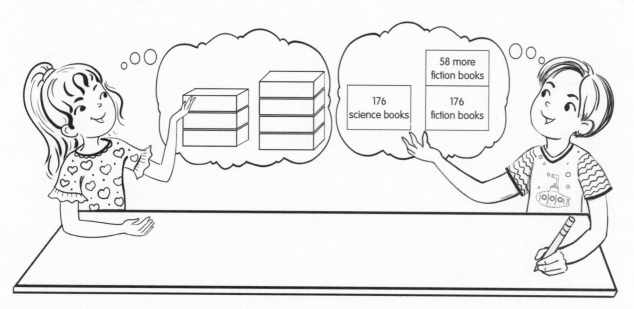

"I get it now," Hannah said. "It's like if I had 3 boxes, and you had one more box than I did. Then you'd have 4 boxes."

"Yes," Carlos replied. "So, the bottom part of the fiction book stack has 176 books just like the science book stack."

"Are there 58 fiction books?" Hannah asked Carlos.

"No, there are 58 *more* fiction books than science books," answered Carlos. "Look, I drew a picture of the stacks of books."

"We have 176 plus 58 fiction books," Carlos continued. "We need to add 58 to 176 to find the total number of fiction books."

"I agree," said Hannah. "Let's add the ones, then the tens. Then we can add the hundred to those totals, like this."

Hannah's Equations

$176 + 58 = (100 + 70 + 6) + (50 + 8)$

$6 + 8 = 14$

$70 + 50 = 120$

$100 + 120 = 220$

$220 + 14 = 234$

"Let's see if we also get 234 by adding 58 onto 176 on an open number line," said Carlos.

"Okay, but I don't know how to start at 176 and jump 58," Hannah said.

"I don't either," admitted Carlos. "What if we try making smaller jumps?"

"So on the number line, we can add 58 in chunks of 25 and 25 for the 50, then 8 more," said Hannah. "Like this."

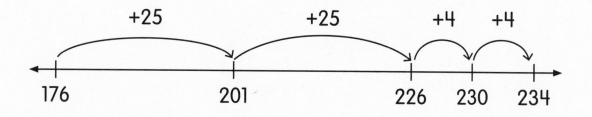

"Yes, and look. We got 234 this way too!" said Carlos.

"Let's make jumps of 25," said Carlos. "I know 75 + 25 = 100. So, 175 + 25 = 200. Which means 176 + 25 must be 201."

"I like how you used chunks," said Hannah. "You pretended 176 was 175 to make it easy to use a chunk of 25. And then you added back the 1 at the end."

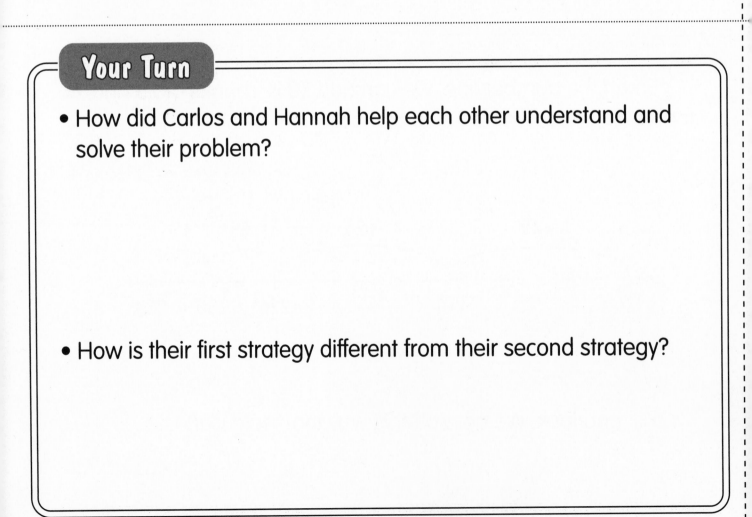

Your Turn

- How did Carlos and Hannah help each other understand and solve their problem?

- How is their first strategy different from their second strategy?

Name: _____

Finding the Larger Unknown

Here are some problems to solve. Try to use the strategies Carlos and Hannah used to solve their problem. Solve each problem in at least two different ways.

1. Amir and Lily jumped rope together. Amir jumped for 59 more seconds than Lily. Lily jumped for 52 seconds. How many seconds did Amir jump?

2. José's family likes to pick apples in the fall. This year they picked 28 more apples than they picked last year. Last year they picked 152 apples. How many apples did they pick this year?

3. The school library has 35 more biographies than poetry books. There are 146 poetry books in the library. How many biographies does the library have?

4. Carlos's family drives to visit their cousins each year. Last year they drove 247 miles to get there. This year they went a different way. They drove 38 miles more than last year. How many miles did they drive on the trip this year?

Extension: Change the numbers in one of the problems above or make your own problem. Solve your problem.

The Notebooks

Solve-the-Problem Mini-Books: Addition & Subtraction © Nancy Belkov, Scholastic Inc.

The principal put 420 notebooks on the supply shelf. She told the teachers to take as many as they needed. At the end of the day, there were 57 notebooks left. Mr. Smith asked his students: *How many notebooks did the teachers take?*

Think

- What is happening in this story?

- What do the students need to figure out?

- What is the important information?

"Okay, I'll pretend to be a teacher," said Brianna. "I take a bunch of notebooks."

"Now let's say I see only 2 notebooks," says George. "I know that the notebooks left plus the notebooks that you took equal 13 notebooks. Since 2 + 11 = 13, you took 11 notebooks."

"I'm confused," Brianna said to George. "We can start with the 420 notebooks, but we don't know how many to take away."

"Maybe if we act this out, it will make sense to us," George said. "And we can use smaller numbers. I'll be the principal. I'll pretend I am putting 13 notebooks on the shelf."

"We can make a diagram using the real numbers of notebooks," said George.

420 notebooks on the shelf in the morning	
? notebooks taken	57 notebooks on the shelf at the end of the day

"The notebooks taken plus the notebooks left must equal 420," he continued. "How can we find how many were taken?"

"Let's start with the 57 notebooks that were left," said Brianna. "Then we can pretend that the teachers put back the notebooks they took. That will tell us what we need to add to 57 to get to 420. Let's say they put back 3, then 40, then 320. I put all those chunks together and see that the teachers took 363 notebooks."

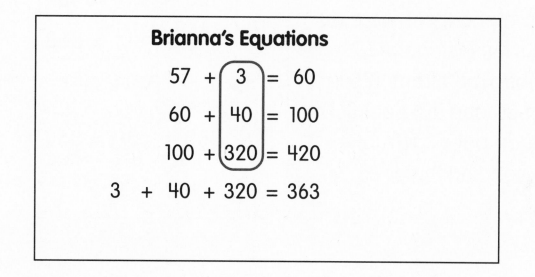

Brianna's Equations

$$57 + \boxed{3} = 60$$
$$60 + \boxed{40} = 100$$
$$100 + \boxed{320} = 420$$
$$3 + 40 + 320 = 363$$

"I like how you added 3, then remembered to take it away later," Brianna said. "Rounding numbers makes math easier for me too. And we got the same answer both ways!"

"Right," said George. "Let's see if we get the same answer by subtracting. We can take away the leftover notebooks from the number we had in the beginning. To make it easier, I pretend there were 60 notebooks left instead of 57. Then I subtract 60 from 420 in chunks of 20 and 40. I get 360. Finally, I add back 3 to make up for pretending that there were 60."

George's Equations

~~57~~ 60 notebooks left

$420 - 60 = ?$

$420 - 20 = 400$

$400 - 40 = 360$

$360 + 3 = 363$

Your Turn

• How are Brianna's and George's strategies different?

• Why do they get the same answer with both strategies?

Name: _____

Finding the Missing Subtrahend

Here are some problems to solve. Try to use the strategies George and Brianna used to solve their problem. Solve each problem in at least two different ways.

1. A librarian put 63 books on a display table on Monday. Kids liked the books and checked them out of the library. There were 37 books on the table at the end of the week. How many books were taken off the table?

2. The first graders made puppets for the school fundraiser. They sold some puppets. When the fundraiser was over, they still had 49 puppets. They started with 132 puppets. How many puppets did they sell?

3. The second graders sold T-shirts at the fundraiser. They started with 215 t-shirts. They only had 38 T-shirts at the end of the day. How many t-shirts did they sell?

4. The students' families baked 230 cookies for a school party. At the end of the party, they had 47 cookies left. How many cookies did people take at the party?

Extension: Change the numbers in one of the problems above or make your own problem. Solve your problem.

Daily Challenge

Jamie decided to run 1 mile every day for a year. She started on January 1st. On her birthday in June, she had 176 days left to reach her goal. Mr. Smith asked his class: *How many days had Jamie already run?*

- What is happening in this story?

- What do the students need to figure out?

- What is the important information?

January

S	M	T	W	T	F	S
✗	✗	✗	4	5	6	7
8	9	10	11	12	13	14
15	16	17	18	19	20	21
22	23	24	25	26	27	28
29	30	31				

"I don't think so," Brian said. "That would be more days than there are in a year. Let's start with an easier problem. After the first 3 days of the year, Jamie would have had 28 more days to run in January. That's less than the 31 days in the month."

"I get it," said David. "She had 28 more days to run in January, because 3 + 28 = 31."

"I don't know how much she's run so far," David said to Carmen and Brian.

"Didn't she plan to run every day for a year?" asked Carmen. "Remember, there are 365 days in a year."

"So do we add 365 and 176?" asked David.

David continued, "So the number of days Jamie's run so far plus 176 will get us to her goal of 365. Just like on this open number line."

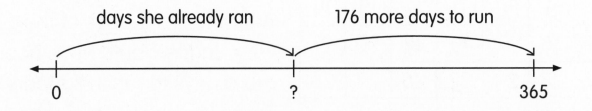

days she already ran   176 more days to run

0   ?   365

"Great! Let's use another number line to figure out how many days she had already run," said Carmen. "I think we can take 176 away from 365. Or we can start at 176 and figure out how much we need to add to get to 365."

Carmen made jumps to go from 176 to 365. She added the jumps and found that Jamie had already run on 189 days.

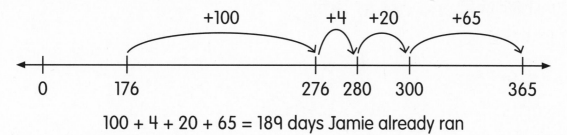

100 + 4 + 20 + 65 = 189 days Jamie already ran

"I used fewer jumps," said Brian. "I know that 25 + 175 = 200. Since we start at 176 instead of 175, I added one less."

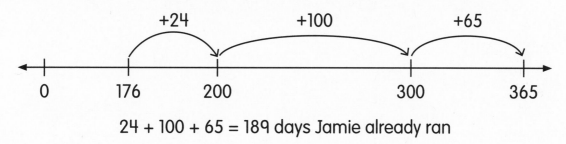

24 + 100 + 65 = 189 days Jamie already ran

"Look! We got the same answer 3 different ways," said David.

David broke 176 into chunks of 100 + 65 + 10 + 1. That made it easier for him to jump from 365 to 176. He took away the chunks on a number line and got to 189.

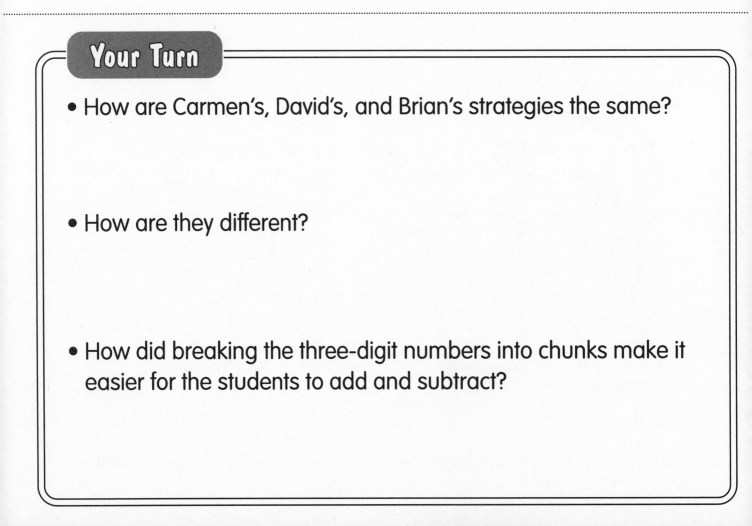

$$365 - 100 - 65 - 20 - 1 = 189 \text{ days Jamie already ran}$$

- How are Carmen's, David's, and Brian's strategies the same?

- How are they different?

- How did breaking the three-digit numbers into chunks make it easier for the students to add and subtract?

Name: _____

Finding the Starting Number

Here are some problems to solve. Try to use the strategies Carmen, David, and Brian used to solve their problem. Solve each problem in at least two different ways.

1. Kelly and her mom rode their bikes 32 blocks on Tuesday. First, they rode to the park for a picnic. Then they rode 17 blocks to get home. How many blocks did they ride to get to the picnic?

2. Anika's grandmother gave her 38 books. Anika put them on shelves with her other books. Then she had 110 books on her shelves. How many books were on Anika's shelves before she added the books her grandmother gave her?

3. On Saturday morning, Jason and Emma started building a fence between their garden and the sidewalk. In the afternoon they added 72 centimeters to the fence to finish it. The finished fence measured 350 centimeters. How many centimeters long was the part of the fence Jason and Emma built in the morning?

4. In September, Trevor's school bought 185 packs of paper. They put the packs of paper with the ones left over from last year. They had 217 packs of paper altogether. How many packs of paper did Trevor's school have left over from last year?

Extension: Change the numbers in one of the problems above or make your own problem. Use a number line to solve your problem.

Answer Key

Title	Answers	Strategies include:
Classroom Visitors (Adding to Find the Result), *pp. 11–12*	**1.** 56 **2.** 57 **3.** 78 **4.** 89	• Count by groups • Add on in chunks of tens and ones • Add numbers by place value, then combine • Draw tens and ones blocks and combine • Add numbers on ten frames
Too Many Stuffies (Subtracting to Find the Result), *pp. 17–18*	**1.** 14 **2.** 13 **3.** 26 **4.** 41	• Draw tens and ones blocks; cross out to subtract • Add up from the number removed to the total • Add on or count back in chunks of tens and ones • Count back from the total to the number removed • Use known doubles to find a missing part
Hatching Butterflies (Finding the Missing Addend), *pp. 23–24*	**1.** 6 **2.** 16 **3.** 15 **4.** 18	• Draw tens and ones blocks; cross out to subtract • Add up to a multiple of ten or add by multiples of ten • Count back from the total to a known addend • Add on from the known addend to the total • Add on or count back in chunks of tens and ones
The Class Fundraiser (Adding to Find the Starting Number), *pp. 29-30*	**1.** 64 **2.** 113 **3.** 143 **4.** 155	• Add up from a known addend to the total • Add numbers by place value, then combine • Add on or count back in chunks of tens and ones • Change into friendly numbers to operate, then adjust • Use known addition doubles
The Tree Display (Finding the Difference), *pp. 35–36*	**1.** 16 **2.** 15 **3.** 34 **4.** 55	• Use ten frames to remove in chunks • Count back from a larger number to a smaller number • Add up from a smaller number to the larger number • Add on or count back in chunks of tens and ones
Canned Food Drive (Comparing to Find the Difference), *pp. 41–42*	**1.** 14 **2.** 37 **3.** 45 **4.** 89	• Count back from a larger number to a smaller number • Add up from a smaller number to the larger number • Add on or count back in chunks of tens and ones
Running Altogether (Finding the Smaller Unknown), *pp. 47–48*	**1.** 45 **2.** 63 **3.** 162 **4.** 84	• Take the difference away from the larger number • Add up from the difference to the larger number • Add on or count back in chunks of tens and ones

Pocket Money (Finding Two Addends), *pp. 53–54*	Possible answers include: **1.** 25 pennies and 1 nickel; 20 pennies and 2 nickels **2.** 18 of one and 22 of the other; 20 of each animal **3.** 6 of one and 16 of the other; 10 of one and 12 of the other **4.** 1 quarter and 11 nickels; 2 quarters and 6 nickels	• Count by groups • Add on or count back in chunks of tens and ones • Use doubles or other known combinations • Use one solution to find the next by adding to one addend and subtracting from the other
Planning a Trip (Finding the Total), *pp. 59–60*	**1.** No. He only has 36 balloons. **2.** 173 steps **3.** 80 pens **4.** 77 minutes **5.** No. He only has 194 pennies.	• Add on or count back in chunks of tens and ones • Add numbers by place value then combine • Use known addition facts to add up or subtract back • Change into friendly numbers to operate, then adjust
Science and Fiction (Finding the Larger Unknown), *pp. 65–66*	**1.** 111 seconds **2.** 180 apples **3.** 181 biographies **4.** 285 miles	• Add the difference to the smaller number • Add numbers by place value then combine • Change into friendly numbers to operate, then adjust • Use known addition facts to add up or subtract back • Add on or count back in chunks of tens and ones
The Notebooks (Finding the Missing Subtrahend), *pp. 71–72*	**1.** 26 books **2.** 83 puppets **3.** 177 T-shirts **4.** 183 cookies	• Add up from the number left to the total • Remove the number left from the total • Add on or remove in chunks of tens and ones • Change into friendly numbers to operate, then adjust
Daily Challenge (Finding the Starting Number), *pp. 77–78*	**1.** 15 blocks **2.** 72 books **3.** 278 centimeters **4.** 32 packs	• Add up from a known addend to the total • Add up with multiples of tens and ones • Remove the known addend from the total • Add on or remove in chunks of tens and ones • Use known addition facts to add up or subtract back